THE PRODUCT MANAGER'S TOOLKIT

METHODS, FRAMEWORKS, AND PRACTICES FOR SUCCESS

Olumide Moses Adedeji

Copyright © 2023 by Olumide Moses Adedeji

THE PRODUCT MANAGER'S TOOLKIT

All rights reserved.

No part of this book may be reproduced or transmitted in any form or by any means, electronic or mechanical, including photocopying, recording, or by any information storage and retrieval system, without permission in writing from the Copyright owner.

Any information is to be used for educational and information purposes only. It should never be substituted for financial advice.

The author or publisher does not in any way endorse any commercial products or services linked from other websites to this book.

Published in Nigeria in 2023

A catalogue record of this book will be available from the National Library of Nigeria.

CONTENTS

PREFACE v
INTRODUCTION viii

CHAPTER 1
Understanding Product Management Fundamentals 1

CHAPTER 2
Strategic Planning and Execution in Product Management 7

CHAPTER 3
Leveraging Market Research for Product Innovation 13

CHAPTER 4
User-Centric Product Design: Principles And Practices 19

CHAPTER 5
Agile and Scrum Methodologies for Product Managers 25

CHAPTER 6
Data-Driven Decision Making for Product Managers 31

CHAPTER 7
Building and Leading Cross-Functional Teams 37

CHAPTER 8
Effective Communication Strategies for Product Managers 45

CHAPTER 9
Navigating Product Launches and Market Entry 53

CHAPTER 10
Scaling Products and Managing Growth 59

CHAPTER 11
Innovative Technologies in Product Management 65

CHAPTER 12
Future Trends and Predictions in Product Management............69

CHAPTER 13
Professional Development for Product Managers 75

TERMS..81

PREFACE

In the rapidly evolving landscape of modern business, the role of the product manager has become increasingly pivotal. As the nexus between engineering, design, and market realities, product managers not only shepherd products from conception to launch but also ensure that these products meet the critical intersections of market demand, technological feasibility, and business viability. "The Product Manager's Toolkit: Methods, Frameworks, and Practices for Success" is designed to equip product managers with the essential tools, knowledge, and insights needed to thrive in this challenging role.

The genesis of this book lies in the recognition of the expanding scope and increasing complexity of product management. As businesses face relentless technological advancements and shifting market dynamics, the demand for product managers who can navigate these changes and drive products that resonate with users is at an all-time high. This book addresses that need by providing a comprehensive guide that covers a wide array of essential topics, from strategic planning and user-centric design to Agile methodologies and data-driven decision-making.

Our contributors, who are seasoned professionals and thought leaders in product management, share their wealth of experience and diverse perspectives throughout this toolkit. Their insights are bolstered by real-world examples and case studies that not only illuminate the theoretical aspects discussed but also provide practical applications and strategies that can be immediately implemented. Whether you are a novice just stepping into the world of product management or a seasoned veteran looking to refine your skills and knowledge, this book offers valuable resources and guidance.

As you delve into the chapters of "The Product Manager's Toolkit," you will discover strategies to enhance your effectiveness in leading cross-functional teams, techniques to harness data for better decision-making, and methodologies to foster innovation and manage growth. Each section is meticulously crafted to prepare you for the various challenges and opportunities you will encounter in your journey as a product manager.

We invite you to use this book not just as a manual but as a companion in your ongoing development as a product leader. The tools and insights contained within these pages are designed to be revisited as you grow and face new challenges in your career. The landscape of product management is one of continual learning and adaptation, and it is our hope that this toolkit will serve you well on this dynamic journey.

Welcome to a comprehensive exploration of the art and science of product management. Let this book guide and inspire you to new heights in your career as you navigate the complexities of delivering products that truly make a difference.

INTRODUCTION

Welcome to "The Product Manager's Toolkit," a comprehensive guide designed to empower product managers at all levels with the essential tools, techniques, and knowledge necessary for success in today's fast-paced and complex market environments. This book is crafted to serve as both a primer for those new to product management and a rich resource for seasoned professionals seeking to enhance their skills and strategic insights.

The Crucial Role of Product Management

Product management stands at the crossroads of technology, business, and user experience, requiring a blend of diverse skills and a multidisciplinary approach. Product managers are not just responsible for managing a product lifecycle but are pivotal in defining the vision for a product, aligning it with company strategy, understanding customer needs, and driving the development process. They act as mini-CEOs of their products, making crucial decisions that can define the success or failure of the product and, ultimately, the business itself.

Given the central role of product management in driving innovation and achieving business goals, there is a significant need for a structured approach to understanding and mastering this discipline. This book fills that need by breaking down the role into manageable elements, each detailed in individual chapters that cover everything from strategic planning and market research to agile practices and beyond.

What This Book Offers

"The Product Manager's Toolkit" is structured to provide a logical progression through the phases of product management, offering insights into both foundational concepts and advanced strategies. Here's what you can expect:

Foundational Skills: Understand the basic principles of product management, including frameworks and methodologies that support effective product development.

Strategic Execution: Dive into strategic planning, execution, and market entry techniques that help in launching and sustaining successful products.

User-Centric Design: Learn how to centre your product design around the user, ensuring that it not only meets but exceeds customer expectations.

Agility and Adaptiveness: Explore how agile and scrum methodologies can make your product development process more flexible and responsive.

Data-Driven Decisions: Gain insights into utilizing data to make informed decisions that keep your product competitive and relevant.

Leadership and Communication: Enhance your ability to lead cross-functional teams and communicate effectively to ensure alignment and promote collaboration.

Each chapter is supplemented with real-life examples, case studies, and actionable advice that can be applied to your daily work as a product manager. This not only enriches your learning experience but also provides practical value, making the theoretical knowledge gained from this book directly applicable.

Who Should Read This Book?

"The Product Manager's Toolkit" is designed for a wide audience, ranging from aspiring product managers who are just starting out to experienced leaders seeking to refine their strategies and methodologies. It is also immensely beneficial for anyone involved in the broader product development process, including project managers, designers, developers, and marketing professionals who collaborate with product management teams.

Your Journey Begins Here

As you turn the pages of this book, we encourage you to engage with the content actively, reflect on your current practices, and consider new ways to enhance your approach to product management. With each chapter, you'll gain not only knowledge but also the confidence to apply these new skills in real-world settings.

Embark on this journey with us to transform your product management practice by leveraging the comprehensive tools and strategies contained in "The Product Manager's Toolkit."

CHAPTER 1

Understanding Product Management Fundamentals

The Role and Evolution of Product Management

Product management blends the art and science of delivering the ideal product that resolves the correct issues for the right people at the right moment. It is a strategic role that balances business objectives, user experience, and technical feasibility to successfully bring a product to life. A product manager acts much like the CEO of the product, orchestrating all phases of the product lifecycle from ideation to market launch and beyond. Their responsibilities are extensive, spanning market and customer research, vision and strategy formulation, roadmap development, feature definition, leading cross-functional teams, and analyzing product performance in the market.

Historically, product management was focused on coordinating production schedules, but it has evolved into a critical strategic role. This evolution is particularly pronounced in the digital age, where software products require rapid iteration and constant feedback loops. Today's product managers must possess a deep understanding of customer insights, sophisticated market analysis, and an agile response to changing technologies and consumer demands.

Frameworks and Methodologies in Product Management

To tackle the complexities of product management, several structured frameworks and methodologies are employed. Agile methodology focuses on iterative development and responsiveness to change, allowing teams to adapt quickly to feedback and changing market conditions. Scrum, a subset of Agile, uses sprints to manage development efficiently, providing regular checkpoints to adjust plans and deliverables. Lean methodology emphasizes creating more value for customers with fewer resources, streamlining processes to increase efficiency and reduce waste. Design Thinking is centred around creative problem-solving strategies that are user-centric, involving users in the design process to ensure the product meets their needs and solves real problems.

These methodologies guide product managers in developing products that are not only innovative but also perfectly aligned with market needs and customer expectations.

Navigating Market Dynamics

Effective product management also requires an astute understanding of market dynamics. This involves thorough competitor analysis, market segmentation, and strategic product positioning. Knowing who the competitors are, their strengths and weaknesses, and identifying different groups of customers within the market based on their unique characteristics and needs are crucial for defining a product's place in the market.

Case Study: Launching Slack

Slack, now a ubiquitous tool in workplace communication, exemplifies how applying sound product management principles can lead to a successful product launch and enduring market presence. Initially developed as an internal communication tool for a gaming development company, Slack quickly pivoted to become a standalone product under the leadership of Stewart Butterfield, the company's CEO.

The Slack team began by defining their user personas with precision. They focused on teams that required constant communication and collaboration, such as tech startups, which often juggle dynamic project demands and require an efficient way to share information and make decisions quickly. The team conducted interviews and surveys with potential users, mapping out detailed user needs, preferences, and pain points. This research highlighted a need for a tool that could seamlessly integrate with other services and provide an organized, searchable interface for communication.

Embracing Agile methodologies, Slack's development team released multiple iterations of the product, starting with a beta version introduced to a limited audience. The feedback from this initial user base was instrumental in refining the product features. Slack's team prioritized updates based on user feedback, focusing on usability improvements and integrations with other tools like Google Drive, Trello, and GitHub, which were critical to their target audience.

Even post-launch, the Slack team continued to enhance their platform based on user feedback and emerging market trends. They implemented features like threaded messages and improved notifications, which were directly requested by users to aid in managing communications more effectively. This iterative process helped Slack stay relevant and highly tailored to user needs, encouraging deeper engagement and wider adoption across diverse teams.

As a result of these focused product management strategies, Slack rapidly gained traction in the tech community and beyond. Its user-friendly design, coupled with powerful integration capabilities, made it an essential tool for teams seeking to streamline communication. By 2021, Slack reported over 12 million daily active users, a testament to its successful product strategy and robust management.

OLUMIDE MOSES ADEDEJI

CHAPTER 2

Strategic Planning and Execution in Product Management

Strategic planning in product management is the comprehensive process of defining a product's direction over a specified time frame, aligning it meticulously with the company's broader strategic goals. This process is crucial as it involves setting clear objectives, pinpointing essential resources, and meticulously mapping out the pathways to achieve these objectives efficiently. This chapter explores various strategic planning methodologies that are essential for product managers to master, ensuring that products are not only launched successfully but also continue to thrive in increasingly competitive markets.

Key Components of Strategic Planning

Strategic planning is built upon several foundational components:

1. **Vision Setting**: Developing a clear and compelling vision that dictates the direction of the product development efforts is crucial. This vision serves as a guiding star for all strategic decisions and development efforts.

2. **Goal Definition**: Setting specific, measurable, achievable, relevant, and time-bound (SMART) goals that effectively support the broader business objectives. These goals provide concrete targets for the team and align their efforts with the overall business strategy.

3. **Resource Allocation**: Identifying and allocating the necessary resources, which include human, financial, and technological assets, required to achieve the product goals. Effective resource allocation ensures that all necessary tools and personnel are available to meet strategic milestones.

4. **Risk Management:** Proactively anticipating potential risks and developing robust strategies to mitigate them effectively. This involves understanding potential obstacles and preparing solutions in advance, which is critical for maintaining project momentum.

Frameworks and Tools for Strategic Planning

To guide and enhance the strategic planning process, product managers can utilize several effective frameworks and tools:

- **SWOT Analysis (Strengths, Weaknesses, Opportunities, Threats):** This tool helps in understanding the internal and external factors that can impact the product's success, providing crucial insights into where the product can leverage internal strengths and external opportunities, while addressing weaknesses and threats.

- **OKRs (Objectives and Key Results):** This framework aims to set and communicate clear objectives and monitor outcomes, fostering alignment and engagement across all team members. OKRs help in focusing efforts and measuring progress towards strategic goals.

- **Roadmapping**: Visualizing the strategic plan through detailed roadmaps that outline the timeline of key deliverables and milestones helps keep the team on track. This visualization aids in planning and provides a clear path for development and strategic adjustments.

Executing the Strategy

The effective execution of a strategic plan is as crucial as the plan itself. Execution involves several critical activities:

- **Communication**: Ensuring that all team members and stakeholders understand and are committed to the strategic plan. Effective communication is key to aligning the team's efforts with strategic objectives.

- **Monitoring and Adjusting**: Continuously tracking progress against goals and making necessary adjustments based on performance data and market feedback. This adaptability is crucial for responding to challenges and opportunities that arise during the development process.

- **Leadership and Motivation:** Consistently inspiring and motivating the team to ensure they remain focused, productive, and aligned with the project's goals. Effective leadership involves encouraging the team through challenges and celebrating milestones to maintain morale and engagement.

Strategic planning in product management is a continuous process that influences every stage of the product lifecycle. From the initial concept to the product launch and through multiple iterations, strategic planning ensures that the product development is consistently aligned with market needs and company goals.

In the early stages of product development, strategic planning is critical for identifying the right market opportunity and defining the product in a way that optimally meets this opportunity. It sets a clear path for the product team, aligning all efforts towards a common goal. This stage involves extensive market research, competitor analysis, and customer interviews, all of which are integral to developing a strategic plan that is both effective and actionable. As the product matures, strategic planning plays a crucial role in sustaining growth and adapting to changes in the market. It involves analysing user feedback, monitoring market trends, and revisiting the initial strategic plan to make necessary adjustments. This adaptability is crucial for maintaining the product's relevance in the market and for seizing new opportunities that arise.

Furthermore, strategic planning facilitates clear communication across the team and other stakeholders. It provides a framework within which decisions are made, reducing ambiguity and increasing the efficiency of decision-making processes. By keeping everyone on the same page, it ensures that the product development process is smooth and coherent, leading to better outcomes and a more cohesive team effort.

CHAPTER 3

Leveraging Market Research for Product Innovation

Market research is an indispensable component of product management, informing each stage of the product lifecycle—from initial ideation through to post-launch enhancements. By providing deep insights into customer needs, market trends, competitive landscapes, and potential barriers to entry, market research equips product managers with the necessary data to make informed decisions. This continuous flow of information helps to shape products that not only meet but exceed the expectations of the target audience. Effective market research is foundational in creating products that truly resonate with users, ensuring that every feature and strategic move is backed by solid data and aligns with real user demands.

The Comprehensive Role of Market Research

Market research is vital for reducing uncertainties and improving decision-making throughout a product's lifecycle. It allows product managers to accurately identify customer needs and preferences, ensuring that the product meets real market demands. By segmenting the market, managers can target segments with the highest potential returns, customizing products and marketing strategies to fit these specific audiences. Competitive analysis is crucial for discovering market gaps and areas for innovation, giving companies a competitive advantage by addressing unmet needs. Additionally, early testing of product concepts before significant resource allocation helps optimize resources and direct efforts toward viable projects. This not only increases the efficiency of the development process but also enhances the product's market fit and success potential. Overall, market research is a foundational element of product management, driving the development of products that are well-aligned with market demands and poised for success.

Approaches and Tools for Effective Market Research

Product managers can deploy a variety of research methods to collect the necessary data:

1. **Quantitative Research:** Utilizing surveys and questionnaires to gather measurable data from a broad audience, which is crucial for validating hypotheses about customer preferences and estimating market sizes.

2. **Qualitative Research:** Conducting interviews and focus groups to gain deeper, subjective insights into the emotions, preferences, and experiences of customers.

3. **Competitive Analysis:** Systematically evaluating competitors' products, sales, and marketing strategies to identify industry benchmarks and innovative practices.

4. **Trend Analysis:** Monitoring industry trends and technological advancements to anticipate future

market developments and align product development strategies accordingly.

Leveraging Market Research Tools

The effective utilization of specialized market research tools is essential for gaining comprehensive insights into customer preferences and market dynamics. Online survey and analytics platforms like SurveyMonkey and Google Analytics are crucial for efficiently collecting and analyzing customer data, enabling informed product development and marketing strategies. Social media listening tools such as Hootsuite and BuzzSumo allow product managers to monitor real-time online conversations, providing valuable insights into consumer sentiments and trends. Additionally, user testing platforms like UserTesting offer direct, real-time feedback from users, crucial for iterative development and product refinement. Together, these tools empower product managers to make data-driven decisions, adapt marketing approaches, and enhance product designs to better meet customer needs and succeed in competitive markets.

Integrating User Feedback into Product Development

Incorporating user feedback throughout the development process is essential for refining product features and ensuring the final product meets market expectations. Strategies for effective integration include:

- **Continuous Feedback Loops:** Establishing systems to collect and analyze feedback continually, allowing for ongoing product adjustments.

- **Beta Testing:** Introducing the product to a select group of users prior to a full-scale launch to gather insights and make necessary improvements.

- **A/B Testing:** Conducting controlled tests to compare different versions of a product feature, determining which one achieves better user engagement and satisfaction.

Market research plays a critical role that extends far beyond merely informing product features; it fundamentally influences and shapes the strategic approach to market entry and growth. By providing valuable insights, market research enables product managers to make pivotal decisions about how products are positioned, the marketing strategies that should be employed, and how to engage customers effectively. These decisions are crucial as they directly impact the product's market relevance and its ability to compete effectively in dynamic market conditions.

Moreover, effective market research helps product managers to understand the evolving needs of their target audience, anticipate market trends, and respond proactively to changes in the competitive landscape. This ongoing process ensures that the product not only meets current customer expectations but is also well-equipped to adapt to future demands. Through careful analysis of market data, product managers can refine their marketing approaches, optimize product features, and enhance overall customer experience. By continuously integrating these insights into their strategic planning, product managers ensure that their products remain relevant, appealing, and competitive, thus securing a stronger position in the market and driving sustainable growth.

CHAPTER 4

USER-CENTRIC PRODUCT DESIGN: PRINCIPLES AND PRACTICES

User-centric design (UCD) is a design framework that prioritizes the needs, preferences, and limitations of end-users throughout every stage of the design and development process. By focusing on the end-user, UCD ensures that the final product not only meets but often exceeds user expectations, significantly enhancing their overall experience. This approach is essential for creating products that are engaging, successful, and truly resonant with the target audience. In this chapter, we delve into the core principles of user-centric design and discuss how these can be seamlessly integrated into the product management process to yield products that captivate and satisfy users.

Core Principles and Techniques of User-Centric Design

The foundation of user-centric design is built on several key principles, each contributing to a thorough understanding and consideration of the user throughout the product development cycle. First and foremost is empathy for users. This involves understanding user emotions, challenges, and real-life contexts through direct observation, interaction, and feedback. Such empathy ensures that the product development team can anticipate user needs and design solutions that genuinely address these needs. Another vital principle is the involvement of users throughout the design process. By engaging users early and often, product teams can gather continuous feedback, which is crucial for validating design decisions and making iterative improvements. This ongoing engagement helps in refining and revising design choices based on real user feedback and usability testing results, ensuring that the product evolves in a direction that is increasingly aligned with user expectations.

Implementing UCD requires a blend of specific techniques that ensure a deep understanding of the user and foster continuous engagement. Persona building is a technique used to create detailed profiles of typical users, which include their motivations, behaviours, and goals. These personas help guide design decisions by providing a clear picture of who the users are and what they need from the product. Journey mapping is another essential technique, where the complete user journey is mapped out to identify pain points and opportunities for enhancing the user experience. Furthermore, usability testing is conducted where real users interact with prototypes and products to identify usability issues and gather actionable insights.

Tools and Strategic Integration of User-Centric Design

Several tools can assist product managers in implementing user-centric design effectively. Sketch and InVision are used for creating interactive mockups and prototypes that can be easily tested with users, providing early insights into user reactions and behaviours. Tools like Hotjar and Crazy Egg track user interactions on websites and apps, offering visual heatmaps of areas where users click, scroll, and linger. These insights are invaluable for understanding how users navigate and experience a product. Additionally, UserZoom and Lookback.io are platforms that facilitate the conducting and analysing of user testing sessions, offering capabilities for both live and remote usability studies.

To successfully integrate UCD into product strategy, product managers should ensure that enhancing the user experience supports the overall business goals, such as increasing user engagement, reducing churn, or boosting sales. This involves collaborating across departments like marketing, sales, customer support, and engineering to ensure that user insights are shared and utilized organization-wide. Moreover, product managers should advocate for user needs in strategic meetings and decision-making processes, ensuring that the product development is continually directed by user feedback and needs.

The Business Impact of User-Centric Design

Adopting a user-centric approach to product design leads to higher user satisfaction and better user experiences, which in turn drive substantial business benefits. Products designed with the user in mind tend to incur lower support costs, achieve higher retention rates, and experience better market penetration. Furthermore, they often lead to increased brand loyalty and advocacy, as satisfied users are more likely to recommend the product to others. By focusing on the user, companies can ensure their products remain competitive and relevant, thereby securing a lasting impact in the market.

OLUMIDE MOSES ADEDEJI

CHAPTER 5

Agile and Scrum Methodologies for Product Managers

Agile methodologies have profoundly revolutionized the landscape of product development by placing a strong emphasis on flexibility, continuous improvement, and rapid adaptation to change. Scrum, a focused subset of Agile, offers a specialized framework that is meticulously designed to manage complex software and product development processes efficiently. This chapter aims to explore in-depth how product managers can effectively leverage Agile and Scrum methodologies to significantly enhance the efficiency and responsiveness of their product development processes, thereby achieving better outcomes in a competitive market environment.

Core Concepts of Agile and Scrum

The Agile methodology is deeply rooted in the principles outlined in the Agile Manifesto, which stresses the importance of prioritizing individuals and interactions over rigid processes and tools, favouring working software over exhaustive documentation, valuing customer collaboration above contract negotiation, and embracing responsiveness to change over adherence to a fixed plan. The fundamental advantage of Agile lies in its iterative development approach, where the requirements and solutions evolve through continuous collaboration among self-organizing cross-functional teams, fostering a dynamic and adaptive development environment.

The Scrum framework, as a prominent methodology within the Agile spectrum, organizes the development process into defined cycles and roles that include the Product Owner, Scrum Master, and the Development Team. It also utilizes specific artifacts such as the Product Backlog, Sprint Backlog, and Product Increment to guide the development process effectively. Key events integral to Scrum, like Sprint Planning, Daily Scrum, Sprint Review, and Sprint

Retrospective, ensure regular progress checks and iterative refinement of the product, promoting a cycle of ongoing improvement that is responsive to user needs and market changes.

Implementing Scrum in Product Management

Within the Scrum framework, the role of the Product Owner is often fulfilled by the product manager, who is tasked with maximizing the value produced by the development team. This critical role involves comprehensive management of the Product Backlog and ensuring transparency and clarity for all team members. The process begins with Sprint Planning, which initiates the sprint by setting the scope of work based on prioritized Backlog items. This is followed by the Daily Scrum, which serves as a dynamic platform for the development team to plan work for the upcoming 24 hours and make necessary adjustments based on the latest developments and feedback.

The sprint cycle culminates in the Sprint Review and Retrospective, where the team collectively reviews the Increment with stakeholders and demonstrates the progress made. This is an opportunity for reflective learning and planning further enhancements, making it a crucial step for continuous improvement.

Benefits and Challenges of Agile and Scrum

Agile and Scrum methodologies offer significant advantages including enhanced flexibility which enables teams to swiftly adapt to changing product requirements and market conditions. These frameworks promote improved stakeholder engagement through ongoing collaboration, ensuring that the product development is closely aligned with actual user needs and expectations. Additionally, the iterative nature of Agile and Scrum leads to higher product quality as regular reviews and adjustments help in early detection and correction of potential errors and mismatches.

However, the transition to Agile and Scrum can pose various challenges. These methodologies require a substantial cultural shift within teams and organizations, which can be difficult to achieve without comprehensive training and management support. The continuous nature of iterations and flexibility can sometimes result in resource allocation challenges, while resistance from team members and stakeholders who are accustomed to traditional development methodologies can further complicate the implementation process. Agile and Scrum methodologies provide robust and flexible frameworks that empower product managers to effectively oversee product development processes. These methodologies not only support rapid adaptation to new challenges and opportunities within the product development landscape but also enhance team dynamics and overall product quality. By adopting Agile and Scrum, product managers can ensure that their development processes are more aligned with modern business needs, promoting innovation and efficiency in product development.

OLUMIDE MOSES ADEDEJI

CHAPTER 6

Data-Driven Decision Making for Product Managers

In today's rapidly evolving and competitive business environment, making informed decisions based on empirical data is crucial for success. Data-driven decision making (DDDM) empowers product managers to validate assumptions, comprehend market dynamics, and refine product strategies effectively. This methodical approach involves the systematic collection, analysis, and interpretation of real-world data, which aids in reducing uncertainties, predicting market trends, and enhancing the precision of product decisions by relying on analytical evidence rather than mere intuition.

DDDM encompasses several critical processes. Firstly, data collection involves gathering both quantitative and qualitative data from a variety of sources, such as user interactions, market research, and operational metrics. This comprehensive data collection provides a holistic view of consumer behavior and market conditions. Secondly, data analysis uses statistical tools and techniques to sift through this data, extracting actionable insights that can significantly influence strategic decisions and innovations. Another key component, data visualization, involves employing graphical representations of complex data sets to clearly and effectively communicate insights to stakeholders, facilitating easier comprehension of trends and patterns that might be obscured in raw data.

Continuous learning is integral to DDDM; as the field of data science is continuously evolving, updating data models and strategies based on new findings and outcomes is crucial for refining decision-making processes over time. This ongoing adaptation ensures that strategies remain relevant and aligned with current data insights and market conditions.

Tools, Integration, and Real-World Applications of Data-Driven Practices

The implementation of effective DDDM is supported by several advanced tools. Analytical tools such as Google Analytics, Mixpanel, and Tableau are indispensable for tracking user behavior and visualizing data trends. These platforms provide deep insights into how users interact with products, aiding in the optimization of user experience and product features. Additionally, A/B testing platforms like Optimizely or VWO enable product managers to conduct experiments by testing different versions of product features to determine which one performs better. This informs development decisions that directly impact product success. Customer feedback tools such as SurveyMonkey and Uservoice play a crucial role in gathering and analyzing direct customer feedback, adding another layer of data for making informed decisions.

For effective integration of DDDM, product managers must establish clear metrics that align with business objectives and provide meaningful insights into performance and improvement areas. Fostering a data culture where decisions are based on data rather than assumptions or gut feelings is essential for aligning the entire organization with data-driven objectives. Additionally, educating and training teams to develop the necessary skills for collecting, analyzing, and interpreting data is crucial for enhancing their contribution to the company's data-driven goals.

The benefits of implementing DDDM are significant and have real-world implications that can transform product development. Enhanced user experience, improved product features, risk mitigation, and resource optimization are just a few of the advantages. By understanding user behaviour and preferences through detailed data analysis, product managers can tailor products more effectively to meet customer needs. Moreover, early identification of potential risks and challenges through data allows for proactive management and solution development, reducing potential setbacks and enhancing product success.

Consider the example of a digital media company that leveraged DDDM to overhaul its content delivery platform. By analyzing user data, they identified that mobile users experienced slower load times, negatively affecting engagement. They prioritized improving mobile user experience in their product roadmap. The data-driven approach not only enhanced user engagement but also increased ad revenue, illustrating the effectiveness of DDDM in making strategic decisions that lead to tangible improvements and product success.

OLUMIDE MOSES ADEDEJI

CHAPTER 7

Building and Leading Cross-Functional Teams

In product development, the skill to effectively build and lead cross-functional teams stands as a cornerstone for success. These teams, which often include members from engineering, marketing, sales, and customer support, collaborate closely to align all aspects of the product with both market needs and overarching company goals. This chapter delves into the nuanced strategies for assembling, managing, and guiding cross-functional teams effectively, ensuring that diverse talents and insights coalesce into successful product outcomes.

Core Principles and Strategies for Cross-Functional Team Management

Effective management of cross-functional teams hinges on a foundation of several critical principles. Establishing clear, shared goals is paramount, as these goals foster collaboration and focus team efforts towards common outcomes. Equally important is the definition of clear roles and responsibilities for each team member, which helps prevent overlap and ensures comprehensive coverage of all necessary tasks. Moreover, robust communication channels are essential for keeping everyone aligned and informed, facilitating a smooth workflow and quick resolution of any issues that may arise.

Building a successful cross-functional team involves strategic steps that go beyond mere assembly. Selecting team members should be based on both their individual skills and their ability to collaborate across different disciplines. Fostering team cohesion is crucial and can be achieved through regular team-building activities and creating shared experiences that promote a sense of unity and shared purpose. Additionally, providing training and development opportunities enables team members to gain an in-depth understanding of each other's roles and challenges, which enhances mutual respect and understanding within the team.

Leveraging Tools and Technologies for Enhanced Collaboration

The efficiency and effectiveness of cross-functional teams can be significantly boosted by leveraging the right tools and technologies. Project management software such as Asana, Jira, and Monday.com are invaluable for tracking tasks, deadlines, and progress across various departments. Collaboration platforms like Slack, Microsoft Teams, and Google Workspace facilitate seamless communication and real-time document sharing, ensuring that information flows freely among team members. Moreover, platforms like Trello or Smartsheet can provide visual representations of project statuses and updates, making them accessible to all team members and fostering a transparent work environment.

Leading a cross-functional team requires a specific set of skills and approaches. Empathetic leadership is crucial for understanding and addressing the diverse needs and challenges faced by team members from different backgrounds and departments. Conflict resolution skills are also vital, as differing priorities and perspectives can lead to conflicts; a leader must be equipped to mediate these effectively. Inspirational motivation plays a key role in keeping the team driven towards common goals, especially during stressful or uncertain times.

Managing cross-functional teams presents unique challenges, such as aligning diverse goals from different departments, which can create friction if not managed properly. Cultural differences between departments can impact work processes, and bridging these gaps is essential for smooth collaboration. Furthermore, competing for limited resources among departments requires careful and strategic management to ensure fairness and efficiency.

A real-life example of effective cross-functional team management can be seen in the strategic approach taken by **Spotify**, the global music streaming service. Spotify organizes its teams into what they call "Squads," which are essentially small, autonomous, cross-functional groups that own different areas of the product. Each squad is empowered to act like a mini-startup within the company, with its product owner, designers, developers, and a dedicated customer support segment. Spotify's approach is particularly noteworthy in how it integrates customer support into these squads. For instance, in developing new features for its Discover Weekly or Release Radar playlists, Spotify included customer support team members directly in the squad responsible for these features. This integration meant that feedback from users about what they liked or didn't like about new playlist features, or issues they encountered, was quickly funnelled directly to the product developers.

By having customer support directly involved, the team could use real-time feedback to inform continuous product improvements. When Spotify users reported confusion about how songs were selected for their Discover Weekly playlists, the product team was able to quickly gather this feedback through their integrated customer support colleagues and adjust the user interface to provide more clarity. They added features such as tooltips explaining why a particular song was chosen, enhancing user understanding and satisfaction.

Benefits of This Integrated Approach

This approach has multiple benefits:

- **Enhanced Product Development:** Direct feedback loops meant that Spotify could iterate on features much more quickly. This rapid iteration cycle allowed them to fine-tune features continuously, leading to a better overall product.

- **Improved Customer Support:** With a deeper understanding of the product features and the rationale behind them, customer support agents were better equipped to handle inquiries and issues, leading to quicker resolutions and a higher level of customer service.

- **Increased Customer Satisfaction:** The swift response to user feedback and the visible improvements in the product led to increased customer satisfaction. Users felt heard, as their feedback had a direct impact on the product's evolution, fostering a stronger connection to the Spotify brand.

This example from Spotify demonstrates the significant advantages of integrating customer support into the product development process. Such integration not only streamlines feedback loops and accelerates product improvement but also enhances the capabilities of the customer support team, leading to better service and heightened customer satisfaction. It underscores how effective leadership and strategic resource management can fully harness the potential of cross-functional teams, driving innovation and business success in a competitive market.

CHAPTER 8

Effective Communication Strategies for Product Managers

Effective communication stands as a pivotal element for product managers tasked with bridging the gaps between teams, stakeholders, and customers. This chapter explores comprehensive strategies and tools designed to enhance clarity and ensure that all parties are consistently aligned with the product vision and progress throughout the project lifecycle.

The role of effective communication in product management cannot be overstated as it often determines the success or failure of a product. Clear communication ensures that everyone involved comprehensively understands the product goals and strategies. This clarity is fundamental in maintaining alignment and focus across various departments. Efficient feedback loops are equally crucial as they facilitate the quick incorporation of suggestions and concerns into the product development cycle, which enhances the product iteratively. Moreover, active engagement with stakeholders through regular updates minimizes surprises and maximizes their ongoing support. To foster this environment, product managers must engage sincerely with team members, stakeholders, and customers to fully understand their views and concerns. This practice of active listening can provide invaluable insights into product development.

Additionally, sharing important information openly builds trust and fosters a cooperative environment, which is essential for effective teamwork and project success. Regular updates keep all parties consistently informed about progress, changes, and decisions, ensuring that everyone remains up-to-date and can contribute meaningfully to the project. Adapting communication styles to suit different audiences—whether conveying technical details to developers or discussing business impacts with executives—is crucial to ensure comprehension across all levels.

Tools and Strategies for Enhanced Communication across Diverse Teams

Several digital tools are available to aid product managers in maintaining robust communication. Email and messaging apps like Outlook and Slack are indispensable for facilitating quick exchanges of information directly or in groups. Video conferencing platforms such as Zoom and Microsoft Teams are essential for conducting remote meetings and presentations, enabling visual and interactive engagements. Furthermore, collaborative document tools like Google Docs and Confluence allow for real-time collaboration and documentation, making it easier to manage project files and maintain a single source of truth.

Communication challenges often arise within diverse teams due to differences in backgrounds, expertise, and expectations. To effectively manage these challenges, product managers must demonstrate cultural sensitivity by understanding and respecting cultural differences that might affect communication preferences and styles. This is crucial in a globalized work environment. Ensuring that all team members have opportunities to contribute to discussions promotes a more collaborative and inclusive atmosphere. Additionally, using clear and straightforward language helps prevent misunderstandings and keeps communications efficient and effective.

Effective communication becomes particularly crucial when managing changes within the product lifecycle. It ensures that transitions are smooth and that all team members and stakeholders are on board with new directions. Properly handling communication during these times minimizes resistance and maintains morale, facilitating easier adoption of new processes or features.

A real-life example of effective communication in product management can be observed in the approach taken by Adobe when they transitioned from selling perpetual licenses for their software to a subscription-based model through Adobe Creative Cloud. This significant shift required not only internal adjustments but also extensive communication with Adobe's extensive user base. Recognizing the potential for customer resistance and confusion, Adobe's product management team undertook a proactive communication strategy. They organized multiple webinars aimed at different user segments, explaining the benefits and logistics of moving to a subscription model. These webinars were tailored to address the specific concerns and benefits relevant to each segment, such as individual creatives, small businesses, and large enterprises.

Creation of Comprehensive Resources & Engaging Directly with the Community

In addition to webinars, Adobe developed a comprehensive set of FAQs that were easily accessible on their website. These FAQs were meticulously detailed, covering potential questions about everything from pricing changes and software updates to how the new model would impact the user's workflow. To further aid understanding, Adobe also released tutorial videos and guides that demonstrated the added value and new features exclusive to the Creative Cloud subscribers, such as cloud storage and regular updates. Adobe took their communication efforts a step further by actively engaging with the user community on social media platforms and through their customer support channels. They encouraged feedback and were transparent about the reasons behind the transition, highlighting how it would allow for more rapid deployment of new features and improvements based on user feedback.

Outcome

This strategic and multi-tiered approach to communication helped Adobe mitigate initial backlash and confusion. By maintaining transparency, addressing customer concerns proactively, and illustrating the long-term benefits of the Creative Cloud, Adobe was able to ease the transition for their users. Over time, the ongoing dialogue helped build trust and acceptance among their customer base, leading to a successful shift to the subscription model. This resulted in sustained revenue growth and a stronger relationship with their users. Adobe's handling of the Creative Cloud transition is a clear demonstration of how effective communication strategies can facilitate major product changes, enhancing user engagement and bolstering the confidence of both the team and the customer base.

The next chapter will delve into the intricacies of navigating product launches and market entry, focusing on strategies that ensure successful market introductions and sustained market presence. Detailed insights will be provided on how to effectively bring your product to the market and achieve a competitive advantage.

CHAPTER 9

Navigating Product Launches and Market Entry

Product launches and market entry are pivotal moments in a product's lifecycle, where meticulous preparation and strategic execution can profoundly influence the success of the product. This chapter explores the essential methodologies and considerations necessary for product managers to navigate these critical junctures successfully and secure a competitive edge in the marketplace.

A successful product launch requires a well-coordinated effort across several key areas. First, market research and validation are crucial to ensure the product aligns with the needs and preferences of the target market.

This involves rigorous testing and gathering feedback to refine the product and tailor it to customer demands. Secondly, a comprehensive go-to-market strategy must be developed, encompassing pricing, promotion, distribution, and sales strategies, all crafted to resonate with the intended market segments. Timing the launch correctly is also critical; it should aim to maximize market impact and align with broader business goals. Furthermore, coordinating all teams and stakeholders is essential to ensure everyone is synchronized and ready to play their part in the launch plan, fostering unity and ensuring that all efforts are directed towards a common goal.

As product managers move to enter new markets, a strategic approach is necessary to capture and expand market share effectively. This involves identifying and targeting specific market segments most likely to adopt the product. Understanding the competitive landscape helps in positioning the product to fill existing gaps or offer unique advantages over competitors. Implementing effective customer acquisition tactics, such as engaging marketing campaigns, strategic partnerships, and influencer collaborations, is vital in attracting and retaining customers.

Utilizing Tools and Managing Risks in Market Entry

Employing the right tools can significantly enhance the effectiveness of market entry strategies. Product management software like Aha! and ProductPlan is invaluable for planning and tracking progress towards launch goals. Digital marketing platforms such as Google Ads, Facebook Ads, and LinkedIn Marketing Solutions enable targeted advertising campaigns that are crucial for reaching the right audiences. Additionally, analytics tools like Google Analytics and Adobe Analytics play a critical role in monitoring online traffic, user behavior, and campaign effectiveness, providing insights that can be used to optimize marketing strategies continuously.

Launching a product and entering a new market inherently involve risks. Product managers must proactively identify potential risks, such as market acceptance issues or operational hiccups, and develop robust mitigation strategies, including contingency plans to handle these challenges effectively. Managing expectations, both internally among team members and externally among stakeholders, is crucial. Clear communication about realistic goals and potential obstacles helps align everyone's expectations and reduces the likelihood of setbacks.

A concrete example of effective product launch strategies can be observed in the launch of the Amazon Echo, a line of smart speakers developed by Amazon. The Echo was one of the first voice-controlled smart home devices to hit the market, marking a significant innovation in the consumer tech industry. Amazon's initial approach to launching the Echo involved a deep understanding of their target audience—tech-savvy consumers looking for convenience in everyday tasks and an interest in smart home technology. Prior to the launch, Amazon conducted extensive market research to understand the needs and preferences of this segment. They also examined the competitive landscape, which at the time was less saturated with smart home devices, providing a unique opportunity for them to pioneer a new product category.

The timing of the Echo's launch was strategically planned to coincide with the 2014 holiday shopping season, a critical period for consumer electronics sales. Amazon leveraged this timing to maximize exposure and capitalize on the increased consumer spending during this time. The launch was further boosted by an invitation-only release, which created an air of exclusivity and heightened consumer interest. Amazon's launch campaign for the Echo effectively highlighted its unique aspects, particularly its voice interaction feature, Alexa, which could perform a variety of tasks such as playing music, making to-do lists, setting alarms, streaming podcasts, and providing weather, traffic, and other real-time information. The campaign focused on how these features could seamlessly integrate into and enhance everyday life, addressing the direct needs and desires of their target audience.

Following the launch, Amazon actively engaged with its customers to gather feedback on their experiences with the Echo. This ongoing dialogue allowed Amazon to continuously refine the product. Over time, they rolled out updates that expanded Alexa's capabilities and integrated the Echo with a wider range of smart home devices and several third-party services. This commitment to continuous improvement helped the Echo remain relevant and adapt to changing consumer expectations, which were crucial as more competitors entered the smart home market.

The initial and ongoing success of the Amazon Echo demonstrates the effectiveness of well-planned product launch strategies. By understanding their audience, strategically timing the launch, executing a focused marketing campaign, and continuously engaging with consumers post-launch, Amazon not only introduced a new product but also established a dominant presence in the smart home industry. This approach has not only sustained the product's market relevance but also fostered its evolution in alignment with technological advancements and consumer trends.

In the next chapter, we will delve into how product managers can scale their products post-launch and manage growth effectively. This will cover strategies for expansion, adapting products to scale, and continuously improving the product based on user feedback and market demands, ensuring long-term success and market presence.

CHAPTER 10

Scaling Products and Managing Growth

Once a product has been successfully launched and begins to gain traction, the next challenge for product managers is scaling. This chapter discusses strategies and tools for managing the growth phase effectively, ensuring the product can expand its market reach while maintaining or improving quality and customer satisfaction.

Strategies and Management of Product Scaling

Effective scaling of a product involves several key strategies that are essential for ensuring sustained growth and market penetration. Enhancing product features continuously based on user feedback and emerging market trends is crucial. This involves adding features that drive additional value and enhance user engagement. Expanding market reach is another vital strategy; this can involve exploring new geographical markets or different customer segments within existing markets, which helps in diversifying the user base and reducing market-specific risks.

Optimizing performance and infrastructure is critical as the product scales. Ensuring that the product's technical infrastructure can handle increased loads is essential for maintaining a smooth user experience as the user base grows. This might involve upgrading server capabilities or optimizing the software for better performance under higher loads.

As the product scales, operational demands will inevitably increase. Managing this scaling effectively requires streamlining processes, which may involve automating and refining processes to handle increased operations without a proportional increase in costs or resources. Enhancing team capabilities is also necessary; this could involve scaling the team strategically to manage increased responsibilities by hiring for key roles and training existing staff to handle more complex tasks. Maintaining robust quality control is crucial to ensure that product enhancements and expansions do not compromise the integrity of the product.

Tools, Technologies, and Challenges in Scaling

Several tools and technologies can assist in managing the scaling process efficiently. Cloud computing services like AWS or Google Cloud are vital as they can scale server resources as demand increases. Automation tools such as Zapier or Automate.io can help automate workflows and integrate various applications seamlessly, enhancing operational efficiency. Performance monitoring tools like New Relic or Datadog provide insights into the performance and health of your product under different loads, allowing for timely adjustments to maintain optimal performance.

However, scaling is not without its challenges. Resource allocation is a significant challenge; balancing limited resources between developing new features, expanding into new markets, and maintaining existing operations is crucial. Preserving the organizational culture and core values despite rapid growth is also essential, as it maintains team morale and company identity. Additionally, as the product gains visibility and enters new markets, increased competition can pose new challenges.

Real-World Application: Scaling a Mobile App

A real-life example of effectively scaling a mobile app can be observed in the strategies employed by **Pokémon GO**. This popular augmented reality (AR) game experienced exponential growth in user numbers shortly after its launch. Niantic, the company behind Pokémon GO, faced significant challenges due to the rapid increase in demand, which put a strain on their servers and highlighted the need for strategic scaling measures. To manage the burgeoning user base, Niantic focused initially on optimizing game performance for a wider range of devices. This involved enhancing the app's software to ensure smoother gameplay across different smartphone models and operating systems, which was critical as the game's AR features required substantial processing power and battery usage.

Simultaneously, Niantic worked on scaling up their server infrastructure. They partnered with Google Cloud to handle the increased load more efficiently. This collaboration aimed to improve server response times and uptime, ensuring that players experienced minimal disruptions during gameplay. The server capacity improvements were crucial for maintaining a responsive and reliable gaming experience as the number of simultaneous users soared. One of the pivotal aspects of Pokémon GO's scaling strategy was the localization of the app's content. Niantic recognized the importance of catering to different cultural preferences and began localizing the game by adding new languages and adjusting the app's content to reflect regional cultural nuances. This not only included translations but also the introduction of region-specific Pokémon, which encouraged more users from various parts of the world to engage with the game.

Additionally, Niantic implemented special events and features tied to local holidays and celebrations, further enhancing user engagement and satisfaction. These events were often tied to specific locations, encouraging players to travel and explore new areas, thus continuously expanding the game's reach and impact. The strategic scaling efforts undertaken by Niantic allowed Pokémon GO to not only manage the initial surge in popularity but also sustain long-term engagement. By optimizing performance, enhancing server capacity, and localizing content, Pokémon GO could accommodate a vast global audience while maintaining a high level of user satisfaction. These efforts resulted in sustained user engagement, with the game achieving impressive revenue growth and retaining a significant user base years after its initial explosion in popularity.

This example of Pokémon GO illustrates how critical strategic scaling is for mobile apps experiencing rapid growth. By focusing on technical optimization, infrastructure enhancement, and cultural customization, companies can successfully manage growth challenges and turn them into opportunities for expanding their market presence and enhancing user engagement.

CHAPTER 11

Innovative Technologies in Product Management

Product managers must continuously engage with emerging technologies to maintain a competitive edge and enhance their product offerings. This chapter delves deep into various innovative technologies that have the potential to revolutionize product management by improving product features, optimizing operations, and enhancing customer interactions.

Among the plethora of technological advancements, several key technologies stand out for their significant impact on product management. Artificial Intelligence (AI) and Machine Learning (ML) are at the forefront, offering the ability to automate complex processes, derive insights from large datasets, and create personalized user experiences. These technologies are particularly effective in areas requiring data-driven decision-making and predictive analytics, such as customizing user interactions on e-commerce platforms where ML algorithms can suggest products based on user behavior and preferences, thereby increasing user engagement and sales.

The Internet of Things (IoT) is another transformative technology that turns ordinary products into smart, interconnected devices that enhance user functionality and experience. For instance, integrating IoT capabilities into home appliances enables users to control these devices remotely via smartphones, adding a layer of convenience and functionality that modern consumers highly value. Meanwhile, Blockchain technology is redefining products that demand high levels of security and transparency. In sectors like supply chain management, blockchain can be used to create immutable records of product origins and handling processes, thus building trust among stakeholders and ensuring the integrity of data across the supply chain.

Integrating these cutting-edge technologies into products requires the use of sophisticated tools and platforms. TensorFlow and PyTorch are popular frameworks that facilitate the development of machine learning models, allowing product managers to harness the power of AI and ML effectively. For IoT integration, platforms such as AWS IoT Core and Microsoft Azure IoT offer comprehensive suites of services that enable the connection and management of IoT devices seamlessly across various applications. In the realm of blockchain, platforms like Ethereum and Hyperledger Fabric provide the necessary infrastructure for developing blockchain applications that can be embedded into products to enhance security and transparency.

Navigating Challenges in Technological Adoption

While the adoption of these technologies offers substantial benefits, it also presents a set of challenges that must be carefully managed. The technical complexity of implementing AI, IoT, and blockchain solutions requires specialized knowledge and skills that may be beyond the current capabilities of many teams, necessitating significant training or hiring of specialized personnel. Additionally, the integration of these technologies often demands substantial investments in time and money, which can strain resources and affect project timelines.

Moreover, market readiness can also pose a significant challenge. The rapid pace of technological advancements means that market acceptance can lag, and users might not be ready for the advanced functionalities offered by these new integrations, potentially impacting user adoption and overall project success.

By effectively managing these challenges and leveraging the right technologies, product managers can drive innovation, enhance product offerings, and lead their projects to success in the ever-evolving tech landscape. This strategic approach not only positions products at the cutting edge of technology adoption but also ensures they meet the evolving expectations of modern consumers, thereby driving business growth and technological advancement in the product management sector.

CHAPTER 12

Future Trends and Predictions in Product Management

Product management is continuously shaped by shifts in consumer behaviour, technological advancements, and evolving market dynamics. As such, product managers must remain attuned to future trends to effectively anticipate changes, drive innovation proactively, and sustain relevance in a fiercely competitive landscape. This chapter delves deeply into the key trends and predictions that are defining the future trajectory of product management, offering insights into how these trends can be harnessed to enhance product strategy and execution.

One of the prominent trends in product management is the increased focus on user privacy and data security. As consumers become more aware and protective of their data privacy rights, there is a heightened demand for products that not only respect these rights but also incorporate robust security features and transparent data policies. Additionally, the rise of AI and automation is reshaping the landscape of product management. AI technologies are increasingly being employed to automate routine tasks such as data analysis and user testing, which frees up product managers to focus on more strategic activities that require human insight.

Furthermore, sustainability and ethical considerations are becoming crucial in product development. There is a growing consumer demand for products that are environmentally friendly and ethically produced, pushing product managers to integrate these considerations into their design and development processes. Advanced analytics tools and predictive analytics are revolutionizing how product managers forecast trends, understand consumer behaviors, and make informed decisions. By leveraging predictive analytics, product managers can not only anticipate market changes with greater accuracy but also adapt their strategies to better meet future demands.

The adoption of Agile methodologies and continuous delivery models is increasingly becoming the norm in product management. These approaches facilitate faster iteration cycles and quicker responses to market feedback, significantly accelerating product development and enhancing team collaboration. As products grow in complexity, the integration of cross-functional expertise becomes indispensable. Product managers are finding immense value in forming diverse teams composed of data scientists, UX designers, and industry experts to develop innovative solutions tailored to complex user needs.

Product managers should also be vigilant about emerging tools and platforms that support these trends. Privacy management tools like OneTrust or TrustArc are essential for managing user data responsibly. AI platforms such as Google AI and IBM Watson provide advanced capabilities to enhance product features and streamline processes through automation. Additionally, sustainability analytics platforms like Sustainalytics and EcoVadis offer valuable insights into the environmental and social impacts of product decisions, aiding product managers in making more responsible and sustainable choices.

Challenges, Opportunities, and Real-World Application

While these emerging trends offer substantial opportunities for innovation and value creation, they also present challenges, including the need for continuous learning and adaptation to rapidly evolving technologies. Product managers must proactively engage in continuous education and skill development to stay ahead of these trends. This might involve participating in industry conferences, workshops, and pursuing relevant certifications to enhance their knowledge and skills.

A real-world application of leveraging these trends for a competitive advantage can be seen in how a leading tech company utilized AI to enhance its customer service platform. By integrating AI, the company not only improved response times and user satisfaction but also solidified its market position by staying ahead of the AI trend. This example illustrates the profound impact that staying current with technological and market trends can have on a company's success and industry standing.

OLUMIDE MOSES ADEDEJI

CHAPTER 13

Professional Development for Product Managers

The field of product management is characterized by rapid evolution and continuous change, driven by shifts in technology, market dynamics, and consumer preferences. This dynamic landscape demands that product managers commit to continual professional development to remain effective and relevant in their roles. This chapter explores a range of strategies aimed at ongoing learning, skills enhancement, and career growth, all of which are essential for product managers aiming to excel and thrive in their careers.

Professional development for product managers encompasses several critical areas. Firstly, it's important for managers to keep pace with the latest technological advancements. This not only involves learning about new technologies as they emerge but also understanding how to integrate these innovations effectively into existing and future products. This continual technological education helps product managers maintain a competitive edge and ensures that the products they manage stay relevant in a fast-changing market.

Secondly, enhancing business acumen is equally vital. This includes deepening one's understanding of business strategies, financial modeling, and market analysis. Mastery of these areas enables product managers to make informed decisions that align with broader business objectives and market needs, thus enhancing the commercial success of the products they oversee.

Moreover, leadership and communication skills are fundamental to the role of a product manager. Developing these skills is crucial for effectively leading diverse teams, managing stakeholders at all organizational levels, and ensuring that all parties are aligned with the project's goals and objectives. Effective communication fosters a collaborative environment, enhances team dynamics, and facilitates the successful execution of projects.

To support these development areas, product managers are encouraged to engage in a variety of educational modalities. Formal education and training, such as pursuing advanced degrees or certifications in product management, business, or related fields, provides structured learning experiences that deepen knowledge and enhance professional qualifications. Additionally, online courses and workshops accessible through platforms like Coursera, Udemy, or specialized product management training programs offer flexibility and a diverse range of topics, allowing product managers to tailor their learning to specific needs and interests.

Attending industry conferences and networking events is another crucial strategy for professional development. These opportunities enable product managers to stay abreast of the latest trends, gain insights from industry leaders, and connect with peers and experts. Networking can lead to new opportunities and insights that are not available through traditional educational channels.

Mentorship and coaching are also invaluable for product managers. Establishing relationships with experienced mentors or coaches can provide guidance, career advice, and insights into handling complex challenges in the product management field. These relationships can be particularly beneficial for navigating the often complex and multifaceted challenges that arise in product management roles.

Additionally, creating a personalized development plan is crucial for systematic growth. Such a plan should include clearly defined professional goals, regular skill assessments to identify areas for improvement, and a realistic timeline with milestones to track progress. This structured approach ensures that learning and development efforts are focused and aligned with career aspirations.

Regular feedback from peers, supervisors, and team members is essential for ongoing development. Structured feedback sessions and performance reviews can provide critical insights into a product manager's growth and development, highlighting strengths and identifying areas where further development is needed. This feedback is crucial for continuous improvement and helps ensure that product managers are always working at their peak effectiveness.

In summary, the role of a product manager is dynamic and demands a commitment to continuous personal and professional growth. By embracing a culture of learning, actively seeking opportunities for development, and utilizing resources effectively, product managers can ensure they remain at the forefront of their field, ready to tackle new challenges and drive product success. This ongoing commitment to professional development is essential for adapting to the ever-changing demands of the product management landscape.

Terms

Product Roadmap Template: A comprehensive guide to help product managers plan and visualize the development timeline of their products.

Feature Prioritization Grid: A tool to assist in evaluating and ranking product features based on their importance and feasibility.

Stakeholder Analysis Matrix: A framework for identifying and managing stakeholders' expectations and influences on the project.

User Persona Template: A template for creating detailed profiles of typical users, which helps in designing user-centered products.

Sprint Planning Checklist: A checklist to ensure all necessary elements are covered during sprint planning sessions.

Minimum Viable Product (MVP): A development technique in which a new product is developed with sufficient features to satisfy early adopters.

Lean Product Development: A strategy that focuses on the efficient development of products with high customer value using fewer resources.

Market Segmentation: The process of dividing a broad consumer or business market into sub-groups of consumers based on some type of shared characteristics.

Stakeholder Management: Techniques and strategies for managing relationships with those significantly impacted by the project or those who can influence the project's outcome.

Product Lifecycle Management (PLM): The process of managing the entire lifecycle of a product from inception, through engineering design and manufacture, to service and disposal.

THE PRODUCT MANAGER'S TOOLKIT

www.ingramcontent.com/pod-product-compliance
Lightning Source LLC
LaVergne TN
LVHW092006090526
838202LV00001B/17